WRITERS' EDUCATION SERIES

ABRACADABRA!

CREATING YOUR OWN MAGIC SHOW
FROM BEGINNING TO END
BARBARA SEULING

To my good friend, Lee Hoffman

Library of Congress Cataloging in Publication Data
Seuling, Barbara.
    Abracadabra!: Creating your own magic show from
beginning to end.
    SUMMARY: Suggestions for staging a magic show, including
tips on creating an image, costuming, and performing, accompany
directions for a number of tricks.
    1. Conjuring—Juvenile literature. 2. Tricks—Juvenile
literature. (1. Magic tricks) I. Title.
GV1548.S35   793.8   75-15629
ISBN 0-671-32740-2
ISBN 0-671-32741-0 lib. bdg.

☆ ABRACADABRA! ☆

Creating Your Own
Magic Show
From Beginning to End

Barbara Seuling is the author and illustrator of more than thirty books for children including *You Can't Eat Peanuts in Church and Other Little-Known Laws* and *The Teeny Tiny Woman*. She has also written a book for adults titled *How to Write a Children's Book and Get It Published,* based on her professional knowledge and years of teaching students of children's writing. For nine years she worked for major publishing houses as a children's book editor.

For several years she served as Director of the Society of Children's Book Writers' New York Conference in Children's Literature, co-sponsored by Bank Street College, and contributed a regular column, "From the Editor's Desk," to the Society's *SCBW Bulletin.* She now serves as a member of the board of directors of that organization.

Her work in children's literature has earned many awards, including the award of the American Institute of Graphic Arts in 1976 for *The Teeny Tiny Woman* and the Christopher Award in 1979 for her work on *The New York Kid's Book.*

She has been an instructor for the Institute of Children's Literature since 1983.

Contents

Welcome To The World Of Magic

Believe it or not, you have already passed the first test in learning to be a magician. You have shown a great interest in magic. (Why else would you be reading this book?)

There is still a lot more to come...about creating a magical character, learning the secrets of conjuring (stage magic), performing some tricks, making trick props...and about putting it all together in a Magic Show.

The Magic Show is what this book is all about. Without doing your tricks for others, what fun would there be in it? A Magic Show is entertainment, making your magic believable, giving people a good time. Your biggest kick will be watching the audience's delight as you perform your magical feats.

So let's get to it right away! We'll begin at the beginning with you—You, the Magnificent.

CHAPTER 1

☆ You, The Magnificent ☆

You are a special person. Of course, you know that. What you now have to do is convince others that you are special. In fact, you want them to believe you have magical powers.

One way to do this is to appear like someone out of the ordinary.

First, you need to create a magical image for yourself. Think of the person you would like to be on stage, performing your magic. Try to get a picture of yourself in your mind. Once you have an idea of who you want to be, dress up the character.

Try on a fancy name. Your own first or last name might suggest a magician's name. Dropping your first name and just using your last sometimes works out well. If it still doesn't sound right, try combining one of your names with one of these adjectives:

wonderful	extraordinary	great
fascinating	fabulous	mystifying
powerful	marvelous	amazing
stupendous	magnificent	incredible

Marvin Kaye, a practicing magician and author of a handbook about magic, goes under the name of

Count Emkay the Miraculous. He got the name from his initials, M and K, and his Count Dracula-type performance.

The great escape artist Houdini took part of the name of a magician who lived before him, Robert-Houdin, and added an "i" to it.

Perhaps the magician Pinetti went a little far. He called himself "Chevalier M. Jean-Joseph Pinetti Willedale de Merci, Knight of the German Order of Merit of St. Philip, professor of mathematics and natural philosophy, pensioned by the Court of Prussia, patronized by all the Royal Family of France, aggregate of the Royal Academy of Sciences and Belles Lettres of Bordeaux, etc.!"

Now that *you* have a name, you will probably find

that you need some stage makeup and a costume to go with your image.

Actors' makeup can be purchased in novelty and magic supply shops, and through cosmetic companies, which are listed in the *Yellow Pages* under "Theatrical Supplies." You can also get excellent results with eyebrow pencils, blue, green or purple eye shadow, lipstick, and other makeup items sold in drug stores and five-and-tens. Maybe you can borrow some.

Cover your face lightly with cold cream before you put on any makeup. This will make it easier to remove the makeup later.

You'll have to practice several times before you know just how much makeup to put on. Beginners tend to use too much, but if you use too little, it won't show up. Try different kinds of makeup; experiment. Stand six to ten feet away from a mirror to see how it would look to an audience.

The traditional magician was usually a man. He often dressed in top hat, cape, and bow tie. This formal look is just one way of setting yourself apart from your audience so that you appear to be someone special. It can be used by girls as well as boys. But if you are a girl, you may want to dress in more feminine attire. Celeste Evans, known as The Queen of Magic, wears a long dress. Litzka Raymond, or The Great Litzka, wears attractive everyday clothes. Gerrie Larsen, The Magic Lady, wears a princess costume, complete with crown.

Boys who wear the formal costume may want to add a mustache and beard with eyebow pencil. Girls may want to wear leotards under the cape and leave out the hat and bow tie. A pendant around your neck would look good. A cloak, or cape, can be made of any large piece of fabric. Just fasten it around your neck with a safety pin. A bow tie can be cut out of cardboard, or a more elaborate one can be made from a piece of cloth, as shown. You can make a top hat out of black construction paper and cardboard.

HOW TO MAKE A TOP HAT

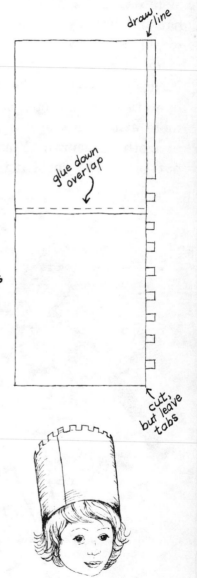

draw line

1. LAY TWO SHEETS OF BLACK CONSTRUCTION PAPER, ABOUT 9 × 12, END TO END.

   OVERLAP THEM ABOUT ONE INCH AND GLUE TOGETHER AT THE OVERLAP.

   glue down overlap

2. DRAW A LINE DOWN ONE SIDE OF THE LONG SHEET, ABOUT 1/2" FROM THE EDGE.

3. CUT ALONG THE LINE, LEAVING A TAB EVERY INCH OR TWO AS YOU CUT.

   cut, but leave tabs

4. ROLL THE PAPER INTO A TUBE TO FIT AROUND YOUR HEAD. GLUE IT CLOSED WITH A ONE-INCH OVERLAP. CUT OFF THE EXCESS.

12

5. STAND THE TUBE ON HEAVY PAPER. DRAW A CIRCLE AROUND IT AND CUT IT OUT.

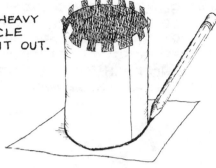

6. FASTEN THE CIRCLE TO THE TOP OF THE TUBE BY GLUING IT TO THE TABS.

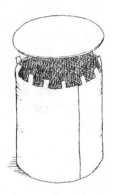

7. MAKE ANOTHER CIRCLE AS IN STEP 5. MAKE TWO MORE CIRCLES ON THE SAME PAPER, ONE 4" LARGER AND ONE 1/2" SMALLER THAN THE FIRST ONE.

BETWEEN THE TWO SMALLER CIRCLES, DRAW STRAIGHT LINES AS SHOWN, ALL AROUND.

CUT THE CENTER OUT OF THE CIRCLE. CUT ALONG THE LINES UP TO THE MIDDLE CIRCLE, TO MAKE FRINGES.

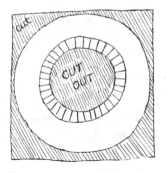

13

⑧ PLACE BRIM ON TABLE. PUT GLUE ON FRINGES ONLY. CENTER THE TOP OF THE HAT ON THE BRIM, AROUND THE FRINGES. LIFT GENTLY AND PUSH FRINGES UP TO STICK INSIDE HAT.

⑨ FINISH OFF BY GLUING A STRIP OF PAPER AROUND THE INSIDE OF HAT OVER THE FRINGES.

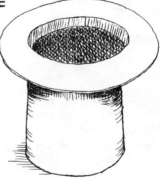

Although the standard color for all of these things is black, use any color you like. Imagine how dramatic this formal outfit would look in bright red!

With only slight changes, you can turn into a vampire. What better way is there to create a

mysterious atmosphere than to have a monster
running the show!

With an eyebrow pencil, draw on bushy eye-
brows and a pointed hairline. Wet down your hair
to make it look slick, let it hang long and stringy,
or bush it out, whichever suits you best. Make your

BEFORE

AFTER

lips blood red with lipstick. Put some green, purple,
blue, or grey eye shadow under your cheekbones
and along the bony areas of your face. This will
give you an undernourished and ghastly appearance. Cheek rouge will make you look too healthy,
so don't use it. Cut vampire teeth out of cardboard.

If you are a comedian at heart, and want to put some humor into your act, perhaps a clown image would fit you best. Simple ideas, like using clothes that are too big for you and a teeny-tiny hat, plus something outrageous—like a big red rubber nose made from a rubber ball cut to fit over your nose, would be perfect. An old stocking over your head would give you a bald look. You can tuck some knitting wool or a torn paper napkin under the sides for a funnier appearance.

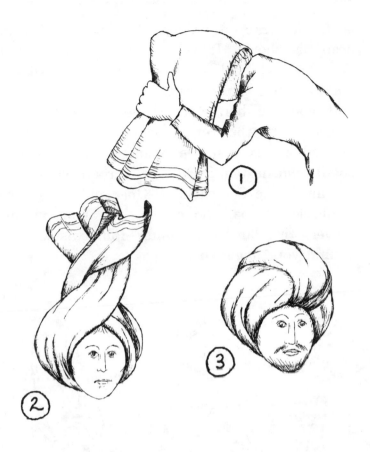

Do you want to appear like someone from the Mysterious East? You can make a turban with a bath towel wrapped around your head and tucked in. With a soft eyebrow pencil or charcoal, draw on a thin black mustache and a short pointed beard. Or wear white pants and a white long-sleeved shirt. Take off your shoes and socks and go barefoot. A girl from the Mysterious East could wear a sari over a short-sleeved blouse and a long straight skirt. A sari is made from one long piece of fabric wrapped around the body and over the head, as shown. If you have sandals, wear them. Paint a red spot on your forehead. Wear many bracelets and tiny earrings.

If you can borrow a jeweled pin from someone, attach it to the very front of the turban. If no jeweled pin is available, you can paint one on cardboard and fasten it to the turban with a safety pin and some Scotch tape. One golden hoop earring would look good, and a big ring. You can make a "silver" ring out of aluminum foil, twisted and bent around your finger to fit.

HOW TO MAKE A JEWELED ORNAMENT

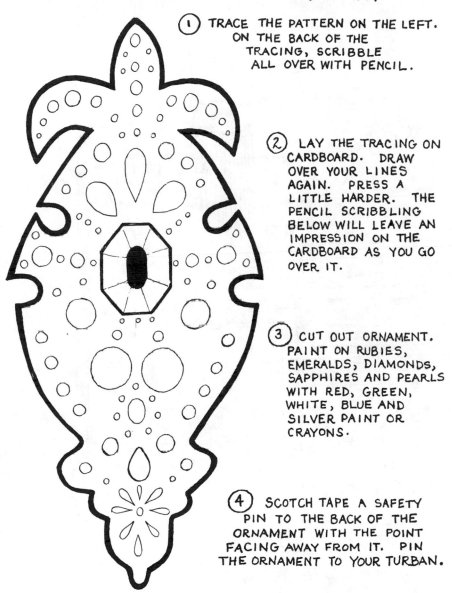

1. TRACE THE PATTERN ON THE LEFT. ON THE BACK OF THE TRACING, SCRIBBLE ALL OVER WITH PENCIL.

2. LAY THE TRACING ON CARDBOARD. DRAW OVER YOUR LINES AGAIN. PRESS A LITTLE HARDER. THE PENCIL SCRIBBLING BELOW WILL LEAVE AN IMPRESSION ON THE CARDBOARD AS YOU GO OVER IT.

3. CUT OUT ORNAMENT. PAINT ON RUBIES, EMERALDS, DIAMONDS, SAPPHIRES AND PEARLS WITH RED, GREEN, WHITE, BLUE AND SILVER PAINT OR CRAYONS.

4. SCOTCH TAPE A SAFETY PIN TO THE BACK OF THE ORNAMENT WITH THE POINT FACING AWAY FROM IT. PIN THE ORNAMENT TO YOUR TURBAN.

If you want to appear old and wise, you can be an ancient wizard. Give your cheekbones a sunken look with some blue or grey eye shadow. Whiten your hair with chalk dust or talcum powder. Make a long white beard out of cotton or a piece of white cloth tattered into strips and held in place with string over your head. A pointed wizard's cap will cover the ends of the string.

To complete the costume, wear a long robe or wrap an old sheet around you. You can paint magic symbols on the sheet to match the wizard's cap. Just fold the sheet in half, make a neck hole, and slip it over your head. The folds will look like long sleeves. You can tie string around your waist if you like.

MAGIC SYMBOLS

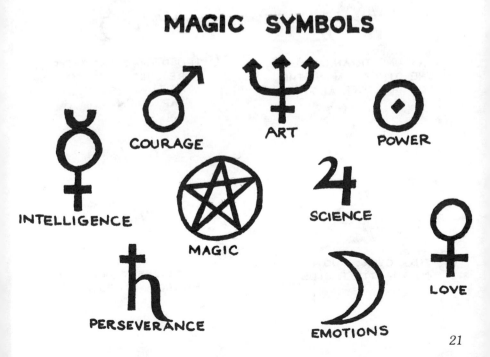

COURAGE

ART

POWER

INTELLIGENCE

MAGIC

SCIENCE

LOVE

PERSEVERANCE

EMOTIONS

HOW TO MAKE A WIZARD'S CAP

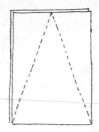

① PUT TWO 12 x 18 SHEETS OF CONSTRUCTION PAPER TOGETHER. MARK THE MIDDLE OF THE TOP EDGE. DRAW LINES FROM BOTTOM CORNERS TO THIS MARK WITH A RULER.

② CUT OUT THE TRIANGLE THROUGH BOTH PAPERS. DECORATE WITH MAGIC SYMBOLS, USING COLORED PAINTS, GLITTER, OR WHATEVER YOU LIKE.

③ LAY ONE TRIANGLE OVER THE OTHER. MOVE THE TOP ONE OVER ABOUT AN INCH.

④ FOLD OVER THE PART OF THE UNDERNEATH TRIANGLE THAT SHOWS. GLUE THE FLAP DOWN.

⑤ TURN OVER. DO THE SAME ON THE OTHER SIDE.

⑥ TRIM OFF POINTS AT CORNERS. HOLD ON TO HEAD WITH BOBBY PIN.

If you don't like any of these characters, invent one of your own. How about a devil, or a witch, or a gypsy? Of course, you can just be yourself, and let your natural self and the effect of your conjuring work its own magic.

If you do decide on a special character, get to know it well. Learn all you can about it. When you plan a show, build it around this character. Wear your costume and makeup while you practice, to see if they are comfortable and if you can do all your tricks in them.

You can add *props*, such as a magic wand, or a crystal ball to any costume. For example, for the wizard, it is good to have an enormous book open in front of you. If you are a vampire, have a drippy candle burning in a saucer on your table.

Another important thing is your *style*. It is the way you talk, and walk, express yourself, meet a situation, handle an emergency, how you dress, your manner of speaking, the speed and rhythm of your movements, your sense of humor, and your attitude toward yourself and others.

It is said that Houdini's brother, Hardini, was a far more skilled magician than Houdini. But Houdini has a more daring, exciting style, so people believed that he was the greatest, even that he was superhuman.

To round out your *image*, bring your natural talents and characteristics to the show. Anything can be of value to a performer. The magician Okito's great-grandfather became a magician because he had a wooden leg that came in handy for hiding props. Colonel Stodare, a 19th century performer, used his talent for ventriloquism in his act. He kept a "talking head" in a box on stage. When the box was carried to the audience, the "head" went right on speaking!

Dancing talent will help you to move around quickly and gracefully during your act. If you are good at gymnastics, you may be just right for escape tricks, like the great Houdini. A quiet or serious manner can put over a mysterious or scientific act.

Bring something to your show that nobody else can—yourself, and your image: your outfit, your delivery, your makeup, your imagination, your program, your style.

CHAPTER 2

☆ A Magician's Secrets ☆

The magic in this book is stage magic, or *conjuring*. There is nothing supernatural about it—it is tricks and illusions.

Tricks fool people because of secret moves and special equipment. *Illusions* are things you think you see but which are really something else. Usually, we see illusions because our eyes play tricks on us.

Pulling a rabbit out of a hat is a trick. The rabbit is hidden, and at the right moment, the magician pulls it out. It only appears to come from the empty hat.

Movies are illusions. We think we see moving images, but the film going through the projector is a series of many thousands of still pictures or photographs. The speed with which they go through the machine creates the illusion that the pictures "move."

In stage magic, everything is planned to amaze and mystify the audience. Miracles seem to happen. You will learn a few of the secrets that make these wonders possible. But you must keep them to yourself. There is an unwritten code among magicians NEVER to tell their secrets.

People like to believe in magic, even if it's only for a little while—like at a magic show. They are delighted to see the mighty laws of nature broken now and then, no matter how. To reveal the magical secrets would destroy that sense of wonder.

If you have assistants in your show, do as popular magician Doug Henning does. Have them sign a pledge of secrecy before seeing all your equipment close up. This pledge makes them promise

Pledge of Secrecy

I hereby promise not to reveal any magical secrets that I may learn during my assistantship, and to uphold and guard the Magician's Code of Honor.

(signed) _____

not to reveal any secrets they uncover while they are your assistants. (Copy pledge on a separate piece of paper.)

Put away your equipment as soon as the show is over. That keeps it from being examined or handled by members of the audience.

Sometimes a friend will pester you for the secret to a trick. Have an answer ready for such emergencies. "I promised not to tell," usually works.

No show can be complete without *props*, or "properties." They are the materials you need to perform your magic. Most of the props you will need for the tricks in this book are easy to find around the house. But you will need some special props, too: a trick glass, a pre-arranged deck of cards, trick paper cups, and others. You can make all of them yourself with simple materials. Instructions are given in Chapter 3. Right now, we will concentrate on a few more general props.

Some people feel less nervous in front of an audience when they are holding on to something. A magic wand can provide that "something" and help you in your magic act, too. You can make one very simply.

Go to the hardware store and buy a ⅜" wide dowel, 36" long. This will cost around 15 or 20 cents. Have it cut down to around 14 inches. Paint the middle part of the stick black and the ends

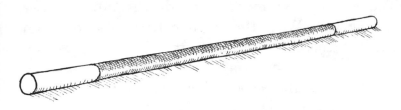

white or silver. Any kind of paint is good for this job, but if you use poster paints they may rub off on your hand. If this happens, cover the paint with clear nail polish or shellac.

A table is important in your magic act. You can use any flat surface, as long as you can stand behind it. Put another small table or chest to the side or behind you. This is to keep your props on. If you have only one table, keep your props on one side of it and perform at the other side.

Have a tablecloth (or an old white sheet) on your table. Let it hang down in front to the floor. Decorate the front with a big monogram — the initials of your stage name—cut out of cardboard and covered with glitter.

There is an old myth that the hand is quicker than the eye. Well, this is not true. The eye can see a movement 200 times faster than a finger can move. But there are ways to trick the mind, and ways to lead the eyes where we want them to look. This is called *misdirection*. When a magician has to make a secret move, he uses this trick on his audience. For a second or two, the audience is led to look somewhere else. This is done so skillfully, that the audience never knows it's happening.

One kind of misdirection is movement. Something moving attracts more attention than something that is still. Always make your secret move

EYES ARE ON THIS POINT

THIS HAND MAKES A SECRET MOVE

with the hand that seems perfectly still to the audience. At the same time, move your other hand to attract attention. Pick up a prop, pull a handkerchief out of your pocket, or scratch your nose.

Another form of misdirection is playing opposites. Convince the audience you are doing exactly the opposite of what you're really doing. For example, to get rid of a crumpled paper in your hand, reach into your pocket to pull *out* a handkerchief. While your hand is in the pocket, of course, you drop the paper. However, be sure you have a good use for whatever you pull out. Otherwise the move may arouse suspicion.

Questions can also distract the audience for a split second. When you have to make a secret move, ask a simple question like "Do you know this trick?" and the audience will shift their attention long enough to answer.

Another trick of misdirection is based on the fact that the audience will look wherever *you* look. If you want to do something with your right hand that they shouldn't see, look at your left hand, or at something else on the table. Don't be too obvious—don't look at the ceiling, for example—or the audience will catch on right away.

Many magicians use *sleight of hand* in their acts. Sleight of hand is trickery with the hands or fingers. It is used to hide small objects when making things "appear" and "disappear." Other names for this skill are *legerdemain* (lightness of hand) and *prestidigitation* (quickness of the fingers).

Not everyone can learn sleight of hand, because some hands are just not shaped for it. You will not need it for any of the tricks in this book. However, you should exercise your fingers and wrists to develop *dexterity*, which is skillful use of the hands.

To exercise your hands, get a small rubber ball —the kind used for jacks, for example—and squeeze it as hard as you can, then relax. Do this often, changing hands. You can do this wherever you go— carry the ball with you.

Now get a quarter or a half-dollar. Follow the illustrations below to learn how to palm a coin. This will make your fingers more flexible. *Palming*

PLACE COIN ON PALM OF HAND. SQUEEZE EDGES GENTLY WITH PALM. FLESHY FOLDS WILL HOLD IT IN PLACE. PRACTICE UNTIL THIS IS EASY AND NATURAL FOR YOU, AND YOU CAN DO IT QUICKLY.

PRACTICE MOVING HAND AND FINGERS WHILE HIDING THE COIN THIS WAY. SOON YOUR MOVEMENTS WILL LOOK SMOOTH AND NATURAL. TRY THIS WITH CRUMPLED PAPER AND A SMALL BALL TOO.

is also an excellent way to make things appear and disappear. If you get good at this, put it into your act to "vanish a coin," as magicians would say.

Your act will also need some *patter*. Patter is the talking you do as you perform your magic tricks. It usually consists of stories that go along with the tricks, or explanations of what you are doing. Patter helps to relax the performer as well as to entertain the audience.

Some magicians prefer as little patter as possible. Others talk, talk, talk. You have to do whatever is most comfortable for you. Try it both ways. If you don't like talking but you don't want a dull show, be silent and mysterious. Let the silence be part of the atmosphere—use lighting and eerie sounds to take the place of talking. If you like talking but don't want to talk anyone's ears off, plan your stories ahead of time. Don't just ramble on. Patter should not have a script, or be rehearsed line for line, but you should have something in mind to talk about when you begin.

You may be tempted to say something like "Here is an ordinary pitcher," because that is what you want the audience to believe. But if an object appears ordinary, and you treat it as ordinary, it will seem ordinary to the audience and not magical at all. So don't call attention to it.

In your patter, remember not to jump ahead of yourself as you explain a trick. Don't tell the audience what you are *going* to do—you will spoil the surprise.

Patter has to be natural and sound like you, telling a story. It should fit the character you are playing. And let the audience hear you: speak up, and speak *to* them. Your voice and your hold on your listeners will be lost if you turn away from them as you speak.

Practice a lot. Know what you are doing inside out. Do every trick in front of a mirror 25 times in a row without a mistake. If you make an error, start all over again.

RULES OF MAGIC

1. Practice.

2. Never tell your secrets.

3. Do not repeat a trick for anyone.

4. Don't tell audience what you are going to do; just do it.

Work at your trick moves until they are easy and natural for you. Memorize everything. Get into character when you practice, by wearing your costume and makeup. It will help you work out your patter and learn to move in strange clothes. Try out your routine on yourself first, to your image in the mirror. Every time you do your magic, try to make it better than before.

If you do your tricks well, you will have the confidence you'll need to do them for others. Every performer needs confidence. Think of the snake charmer of India. His act consists of luring deadly snakes out of baskets with his flute-playing, and then luring them back in again. If he hesitated for one second, chances are he would not be around to perform a second time—the snakes would see to that.

Well, there's no real harm that can come to you for blowing your act. Audiences have stopped throwing tomatoes at bad performers in our times. But if you want a good reputation as a magician, you'd better be good at your work.

Now that you know a magician's secrets, and are sworn by honor not to reveal them, you are ready to learn some tricks and illusions. In them lie the most fascinating secrets of all.

CHAPTER 3

Your Bag Of Tricks–Some Warm-Ups And Relaxers

Every magician has a collection of favorite tricks or illusions. Most magicians find that there is one trick or one kind of trick that fascinates them most, and they will work to improve on it until it bears their own personal touch. The famous magicians of the past are generally identified with such favorites.

Harry Houdini, for example, was a master of illusion in the early part of this century, and was best known for his escape tricks. He would lock himself into trunks, seal himself in bags or boxes, chain himself inside safes, and have himself bound and submerged in water—and always escape.

The great Thurston had a spectacular act, pulling silver dollars out of the air one after another until he filled a bucket with them.

John Scarne has devoted his life to being clever with cards and is perhaps the world's greatest authority on card trickery. He has often been called on to help expose crooked gambling casinos and cheats.

Many magicians have made things vanish, but the great Blackstone perfected the illusion. He made a bird cage disappear while a member of the audience held it!

It may be a while before you specialize. In the meantime, learn the following tricks and illusions. They are based on principles that have astounded audiences for centuries. If you learn them well, you will have all the basic skills necessary to be a magician.

When you have mastered these magical routines, there are books that will teach you more. A bibliography at the end of the book lists some of them. Your neighborhood librarian can help you.

There are also ready-made tricks available from magic supply shops. These often come in packages with routines already worked out, and even with suggestions for music, costuming, and patter. However, these cost money, and are usually no better than the tricks you can get from books or perhaps from your own imagination.

The simplest tricks are always the best ones. They are usually the ones that have lasted through the centuries. And remember, no matter how simple

HOW TO LEARN A NEW TRICK

1. Read through instructions for a general understanding.

2. Read over again. This time make all props.

3. Go through it from beginning to end, using props.

4. Repeat until you have memorized all moves.

5. Do the trick 25 times perfectly in front of a mirror. If you make a mistake, start counting all over again.

a trick may seem to you, it is probably new to your audience.

On 3″ x 5″ index cards, keep a record of the tricks you learn and like. Put down the name of the trick, the props you will need, and any suggestions you have for patter. Note also when and for whom you performed the trick, and leave space for comments about the audience's reaction. This will help you later on when you are selecting material for a show.

THE MAGIC CYLINDER

Trick : Make a coin vanish and reappear.

Secret: Fake rim on glass covers coin when glass rests on matching paper.

Props: glass, white paper, glue, coin

Patter: Uncle Willy, a prison guard, used to try cheering up prisoners with this trick, but it never worked. Maybe because he used a tin cup instead of a glass!

2/4/75 – few friends, my room – good reaction

3/16/75 – after dinner in playroom, family + friends. Baffled everyone.

3/25/75 – classroom in school – kids in back couldn't see coin. Use half dollar instead of nickel.

39

These first few tricks and illusions are good for warming up an audience at the beginning of a show. They also work well to fill gaps between more complicated tricks. They are easy and fun, and give you a short rest without stopping your show.

The Rubber Pencil

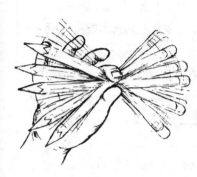

You can make an ordinary pencil look as if it turned to rubber. Hold the pencil very loosely between the second joint of your index finger and your thumb. Move your arm up and down rapidly, from the elbow, in short jerks. The pencil will give the illusion that it can bend. Do this one in front of a mirror. You can see the results yourself.

The Sausage on the End of Your Nose.

Bring your two index fingers together in front of and above the tip of your nose, at a distance of about two inches away. Keep your eyes on the spot where the fingers join and move your fingertips slowly, even closer to your nose. You will find that you are holding a sausage between your fingertips. This is an illusion you can do perfectly on your first try. In fact, the whole audience can do it with you during your show.

The Paper Race

Ask for a volunteer from the audience. You are going to race the volunteer in tearing a piece of paper into three parts. Have two pieces of paper, about 8 x 11, torn in two places as shown, to "get it started." Hand one sheet to the volunteer and state the rules. You must hold the paper with both hands by the upper corners, while keeping your hands in place until the paper is divided. The volunteer will not be able to tear it into thirds. Then you do it. The secret is: *hold the middle section in your teeth and tear straight downwards with your hands!*

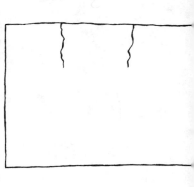

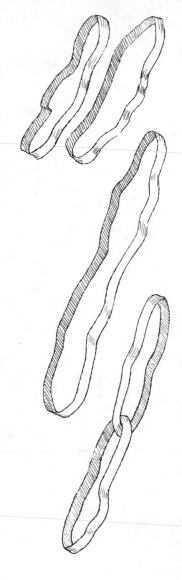

The Afghan Bands

Cut three strips of newspaper about 2 inches wide and about 4 feet long. (You will have to glue some together in advance to get the strips long enough.) Paste the ends of each band together beforehand. Paste the first one in the regular way. With the second band, twist one end of the strip once before pasting it to the other end. With the third, twist one end *twice* before pasting it to the other end. Then later, in front of your audience, cut the rings in half the long way. The first will come out as two narrow bands. The second will come out as one very long ring. The third will come out as two narrow bands linked together. The secret is not to let the audience know that you have twisted the bands during the pasting.

Paper Rabbits

Everyone loves rabbits, and rabbits are always associated with magic. Here are some different rabbits that will amuse everyone.

42

It is done by paper-cutting, and will keep your hands from fidgeting if you are nervous. After a few times, you won't even need a pattern to cut from.

Fold a piece of paper in half. Fold it in half in the same direction again. (The more times you fold the paper, the more rabbits you get.)

Keeping the folded paper closed, draw the pattern below onto your first fold. Be sure the rabbit's nose is on the fold. After you practice the drawing a few times, you will be able to do it more easily. The outline is made up of a few simple lines—the face and the top of the arm make a number 2, for example. And from the arm to the leg is a letter "C." It doesn't matter if the drawing is not perfect—as long as you put long ears on it, they'll look like rabbits!

Cut along the lines. Open up the folds. Rabbits!

As you cut out the paper rabbits—but before the audience knows what you're doing—you might say that all magicians who are worth

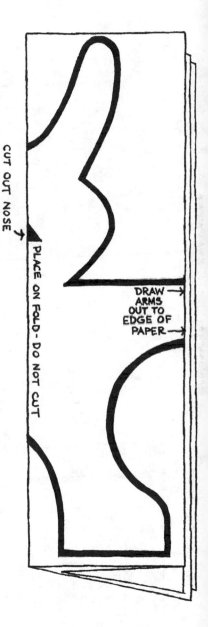

anything pull out a rabbit before the show is over. Well, your mother, (or brother, sister, uncle, aunt) is allergic to rabbits—so these will have to do. Just at that point, open up your string of paper rabbits. Hand them to someone in the audience.

A suggestion: cut out just two paper rabbits—a Mama and a Papa —early in your show. Later on, cut out the rest of the family— four or eight tiny paper rabbits.

The Tree of Life

This is a dramatic presentation if you need something showy. Take six sheets of newspaper and roll them up one after another, overlapping each sheet as you roll, as shown. Flatten the tube of newspapers and make four six-inch tears down from the rim. Squeeze into tube shape again. Let the torn flaps hang down the sides of the

OVERLAP THE SHEETS

44

tube. Put your finger down inside the tube and grasp the innermost roll, and pull gently; slide the paper up, up, up, twisting a little as it comes up. The tree will grow taller and taller, probably taller than you are. So be sure your

LIFT AND TWIST
GENTLY WITH YOUR
INDEX FINGER.

ceiling is high enough for this act! Do not use more than six sheets of newspaper, or else the tube will be too hard to tear.

45

Egg-Spinners

Ask several members of the audience to come up to the table and spin an egg, one at a time. Hand them each an egg out of a bowl or a basket as they come up. Be sure they are fresh *raw* eggs. They will not spin. After several tries, pick up an egg yourself (but make sure this one is *hard-boiled*) and spin it. It will spin, and your audience will be amazed. Of course, beforehand, you will have to mark the hard-boiled egg in some way that your audience won't see—perhaps a pinhole punched at one end. Or maybe you can keep track of the egg by placing it where you can pick it out from the rest.

CHAPTER 4

Your Bag of Tricks—
Razzlers and Dazzlers

The Magic Cylinder

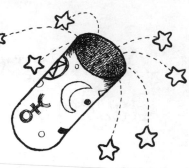

The Trick: Under the magic cylinder, a coin disappears and reappears again!

The Secret: A secret lid over the rim of the glass conceals the coin. When the glass is lifted, the coin seems to reappear.

Props and Preparation:

Materials

    a glass
    a coin, larger than a dime
    a piece of construction paper, 8″ x 11″
    2 pieces of white typing paper, 8″ x 11″
    glue
    scissors
    pencil

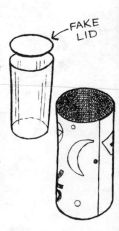

Glass With Secret Lid — Cut a circle out of one sheet of white paper to fit the rim of the glass. Glue it to the rim. Trim off any overlapping paper.

Magic Cylinder — Decorate the heavy paper with magic symbols. Roll it into a tube large enough to fit over the glass, with the symbols showing on the outside. Glue the paper closed.

Doing Your Magic:

1. Rest the glass and the cylinder on one sheet of white paper, as shown. Hold up the coin to your audience, then place it on the paper in front of the glass and cylinder.

2. Lift the cylinder and place it over the glass. Pressing the cylinder against the glass, lift and place over the coin.

3. Lift off the cylinder, without the glass, and—the coin is gone! Actually, the fake lid on the glass conceals it.

4. Place the cylinder back over the glass. Again, lift the glass with the cylinder. The coin reappears!

Tip: Do not lift the glass without using the cylinder, or the fake lid will show. When resting on the white paper, the lid will not show.

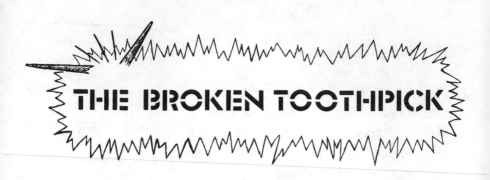

THE BROKEN TOOTHPICK

The Trick: A toothpick, wrapped in a handkerchief, is broken in two. Shake out the handkerchief and the toothpick falls out unbroken!

The Secret: A second toothpick, hidden beforehand in the hem of the handkerchief, is the one that is broken. The one wrapped up is never harmed.

Props and Preparation:

Materials
    two toothpicks
    a handkerchief or kerchief with a hem

Before the performance, slide one toothpick into the hem of the handkerchief near a corner where it won't show.

toothpick is hidden in hem

Tip: Keep track of the hidden toothpick and be sure this is the one that is broken.

Doing Your Magic:

1. Lay the handkerchief out flat. Hold the corner with the hidden toothpick under the fingers of your right hand.

"I have here a handkerchief..."

2. Show the other toothpick to the audience. Place it on the handkerchief.

"and this, as you can see, is a toothpick."

3. Wrap up the toothpick in the handkerchief. Let the loose toothpick fall to the left and bottom fold while you skillfully move the hidden toothpick toward the center top of the handkerchief.

"I shall now wrap this toothpick in the handkerchief."

4. Feeling the toothpick beneath the folds, ask someone from the audience to break the toothpick in two. (Be sure you hold up the secret one to break.) You will hear the snap. The audience will agree that the toothpick is broken.

"Now who will break the toothpick so that everyone will hear it snap? ...Thank you."

5. Wave a magic wand over the handkerchief. Say a magic word. ABRACADABRA! Shake out the handkerchief and the whole toothpick drops to the floor. (The toothpick in the hem, now broken, remains hidden.)

"A simple magic word - ZOX!- and the toothpick is all in one piece again."

ᴛHᴇ ᴍYSᴛIᴄᴀL ᴇYᴇ

The Trick: The swinging pendulum mysteriously answers your most secret questions!

The Secret: Nobody knows why this works, but it does. There is a pulse in the tip of the thumb—perhaps it works like a lie detector.

Props and Preparation:

Materials

> a 12-inch string
> a weight (a stone, a light fishing sinker, a spool, a small rubber ball, a marble)
> glue

Tie or glue one end of the string to the weight.

Doing Your Magic:

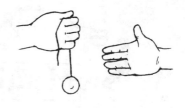

1. Hand the mystical eye pendulum to someone in the audience. Ask that person to hold the end of the string with his thumb and forefinger and to hold it very still.

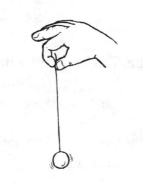

2. Ask the person some questions, but tell him not to answer. The Mystical Eye Pendulum will answer for him: toward and away from the body for "yes," and from left to right for "no." No matter how steady he keeps his hand, the "eye" will move to answer questions.

DO YOU LIKE ICE CREAM?

Tip: Ask any questions as long as it's all in fun. For example, you can ask a friend: "Do you like to kiss girls (or boys)?" Or, "Do you still sleep with a teddy bear?"

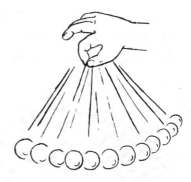

Magic Spelling

The Trick: You take all the cards of one suit out of the deck, turn them face down, and start spelling with some amazing results!

The Secret: The cards are in a special order before you start for this to work out. Even so, it's quite spectacular.

Props and Preparation:

Materials

a deck of cards

Before your performance, take all the hearts (or any other suit you prefer) out of the deck. Put the cards in this order:

5-9-10-King-Jack-2-4-6-Queen-Ace-7-8-3

Hold the packet of hearts face down. The 5 should be on top of the packet. Put the cards back into the deck in this same order, in between other cards.

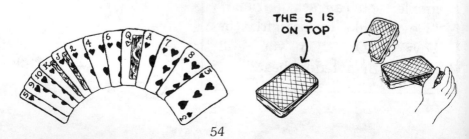

THE 5 IS ON TOP

Doing Your Magic:

1. Go through the deck of cards, face up, and take out all the hearts. (Since the deck has been pre-arranged, the cards will come out in the right order for your trick.) Hold the packet of hearts face down.

2. Begin to spell out the value of all the cards in the packet of hearts. (A-C-E, T-W-O, and so on). For each letter you call out, take a card from the top of the packet and slip it underneath the packet. Turn up the next card after spelling out each card's name. This card will always be the one you have just finished spelling, right through to the King.

"FIRST LET'S TAKE ALL THE CARDS OF ONE SUIT – HEARTS FOR INSTANCE – OUT OF THE DECK."

"NOW I'LL PLACE ALL THE HEARTS RIGHT HERE ON THE TABLE..."

"AND SHOW YOU SOME MAGIC SPELLING."

"A·C·E , T-W-O, T·H·R·E·E, etc."

THE PHANTOM MONEY BOX

The Trick: You put a penny in an empty box, cover it, shake it, and the penny multiplies!

The Secret: Under a false lid inside the box top, there are many pennies stuck there with wax. The shaking loosens them, and they seem to come from nowhere.

Props and Preparation:

Materials

a box with a lid
  (the type that candy
  or gifts come in)
markers or paints
a piece of white cardboard
  at least as big as the box

a candle
a match
about 15 pennies

Money Box with Trick Lid—Decorate the box with the colored markers. Use magical symbols, dollar signs, or whatever you like. Cut out a piece of cardboard to fit inside the box lid. It should fit loosely enough to drop into the lower part of the box without catching. It must be of the same color as the inside of the box.

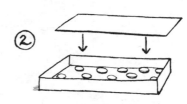

Hidden Pennies—With a bit of melted wax, stick the pennies (except one) to the inside of the real box lid. Put the fake lid over the pennies.

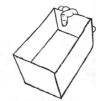

Doing Your Magic:

1. Have the box lid, inside showing, on the table near the box.

2. Show the box bottom to the audience to prove that it is empty.

3. Put a penny in the empty box.

4. Lift up the lid carefully, tilting it *toward* you, and place it on the box.

5. Shake the box up and down until you hear a lot of rattling and all the pennies have had a chance to drop.

6. Take the lid off the box and lay it face down on the table.

7. Show the box full of pennies to the audience.

> **Tip:** When you lift up the box lid, be careful not to shake the pennies loose too soon.

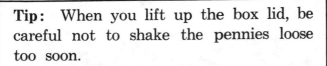

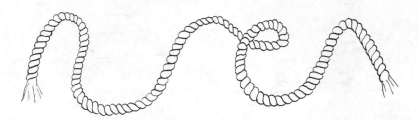

The Great Rope Escape

The Trick: Slip out of a rope and mystify the audience!

The Secret: A simple move is the whole secret to this trick.

Props and Preparation:

Materials

  a handkerchief
  a piece of rope about 6 feet long

Learn the moves well and that's all the preparation you'll need.

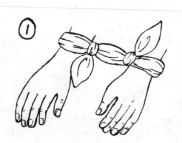

Doing Your Magic:

1. Have someone from the audience tie your wrists with the handkerchief, as shown. Your hands should be slightly separated. Do not cross your wrists.

2. Have the volunteer pass the rope between your wrists and pull the rope so that the center is between your wrists while she holds the ends. Tell her to hold them tight so you can't escape.

3. Turn away from the audience. As you do, hold the rope by its center with your left hand and pass the center between your right wrist and the handkerchief, toward your fingers.

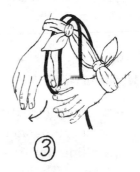

4. When the loop is big enough, slip it over your hand. Pull the rope up as shown and you will be free. Just as you pull free, turn back to the audience and drop the rope. Your wrists are still tied with the handkerchief, and the volunteer is still holding the ends of the rope. Your audience will be baffled.

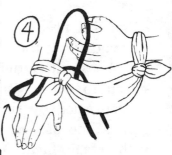

Tip: Don't stay turned away from your audience too long!

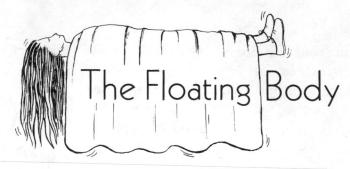

The Floating Body

The Trick: A body rises in the air without help from anyone!

The Secret: An assistant holds fake feet on poles while her back rests on a chair and her real feet are on the floor. To rise, she raises and lowers herself.

Props and Preparation:

Materials

> 2 poles (yardsticks, broom handles, etc.)
> socks and shoes (of floating person)
> stuffing for feet
> tape (the stronger the better—like adhesive or cloth)
> sheet
> chair

You will need two assistants—one to "float" and one to help you carry the "body" on and off stage. Fill the socks and shoes with stuffing (newspaper, rags, and so forth.) Attach to poles with tape. Be sure the stuffing and tape are concealed by the socks and the feet look natural.

Have one of your assistants place a chair in the center of the stage, facing forward. Leave plenty of room in front of the chair.

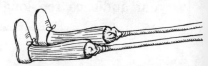

Doing Your Magic:

1. You and an assistant carry out a horizontal "sleeping" person, covered by a sheet from the neck to the ankles.

   What's really happening: "Sleeper" walks backward, carrying poles with fake feet attached under her arms. Assistant at feet end pretends to support lower half of body. You direct the sleeper, who cannot see.

2. The sleeper is placed, horizontally, on the chair.

   What's really happening: Sleeper's back is on the chair; her feet are on the floor.

3. Slowly, the body begins to rise. Then it settles down again.

   What's really happening: Sleeper "sits up," but keeps her head back as though still lying down. Then she comes down again.

4. The assistants carry the sleeping person off stage in the same manner as before, in step 1.

Tip: Be sure the "sleeper" you choose can do these difficult moves.

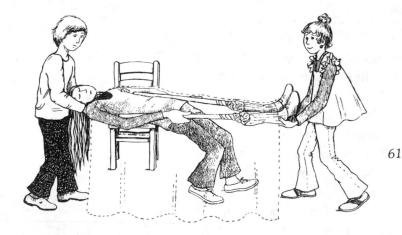

61

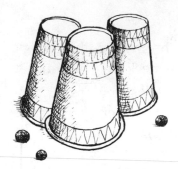

THE AMAZING CUPS AND BALLS

The Trick: Before your eyes, three balls pass through the cups!

The Secret: A fourth ball is the secret to the whole cups and balls routine.

Props and Preparation:

Materials

3 paper cups

4 tiny balls, about ¼" in diameter, cut from an old sponge

SECRET BALL IS IN THE MIDDLE CUP

Before you go on, stack the cups, one into the other, mouth up. Place the secret fourth ball in the middle cup.

Tip: You must be able to move the cups so that it looks like there is nothing in them, even when there is. When taking a cup from the bottom of the stack, move it down, to the right, and up and over with a swoop. Practice this move carefully before proceeding.

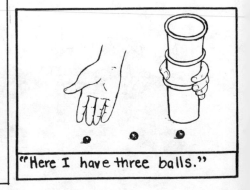

"Here I have three balls."

Doing Your Magic:

1. Pick up the three balls in your right hand and the three cups in your left. Place the balls side by side on the table.

2. Take the bottom cup in your right hand and put it, mouth down, behind the first ball on the table. Put the middle cup behind the middle ball, and the last cup behind the third ball. (When you do this, the secret ball will fall onto the table under the middle cup.)

3. Pick up any one of the balls and place it on the middle cup.

4. Pick up either of the remaining cups and drop it over the middle cup with the ball on it. Drop the last cup over the other two.

5. Order the ball to "PASS!" as you tap your fingers on the cups.

6. Lift the stack of cups. The ball is on the table. It seems to have passed through the cup.

7. Give the top cup to someone in the audience to examine. As you do, tilt the two cups in your hand to let the secret ball slide into your fingers. Get rid of it when you put the other balls into your pocket.

"Here I have 3 balls and 3 cups."

"Now watch. I am going to put this ball on this cup."

"Now I will cover it with the other two cups."

"Now I will order the ball to PASS!"

"And here it is!"

63

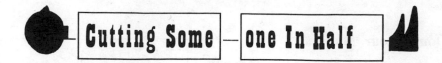 **Cutting Some** — **one In Half**

The Trick: Cut someone in half with ropes!

The Secret: A small piece of white thread holds the ropes
together in the center. When the ropes are pulled, the
thread breaks and they slide around the "victim's"
body. It looks as if the ropes go right through.

Props and Preparation:

Materials

> two 6-foot lengths of rope
> cotton thread (the kind that breaks easily)

Tie the two ropes together at the center, with the piece
of thread.
Your assistant should be on stage with you.

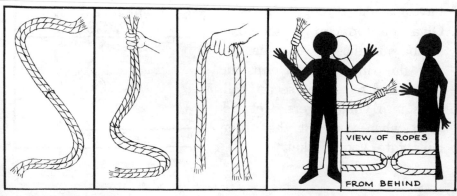

VIEW OF ROPES

FROM BEHIND

Doing Your Magic:

1. Lay the ropes side by side on the floor.

2. Show the ropes to the audience. Hold them up by the ends—the thread won't show.

3. Pick up the ropes by the centers. Your hand will cover the thread.

4. Have a volunteer come up and stand next to your assistant. Go *behind* your assistant, take two ends of the *same* rope, and hand them to the volunteer.

5. Hold the other two ends yourself and stand on the other side of your assistant.

6. Take one of your rope ends and one of the volunteer's rope ends and make a half knot. Give *your* end to the volunteer and you keep the other end.

7. Tell the volunteer to hold the ropes very tight. Count 1 . . . 2 . . . 3. On the count of 3, pull hard. (Your assistant can let out a small scream here.) It will look as if the ropes have cut right through your assistant's body.

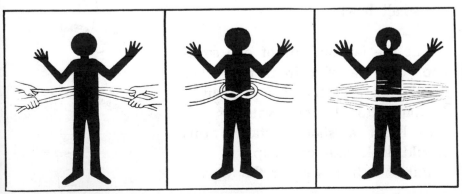

The Magical  Milkshake

The Trick: As you pour chocolate milk back and forth between cups, it changes into a chocolate bar!

The Secret: The smaller cup is actually made of two cups, one rimless and one bottomless. Placed one inside the other, they look like one cup. In a clever move, the part containing the milk is hidden in the large cup. The other (empty) part is "vanished" with magic dust and in its place you produce a candy bar.

Props and Preparation:

Materials

    pitcher containing about 1 cup of chocolate milk
    2 small paper cups
    1 large paper cup, the type that
       big thick shakes come in
    medium-sized paper bag
    chocolate bar
    rubber band
    small bowl

Cut the bottom out of one small cup. Cut the rim from the other small cup. Slip the one without a bottom into the one without the rim. From a short distance, this should look like one cup.

Put the chocolate bar flat on the

bottom of the paper bag. Fold the bag flat and then in half across its center. Have it on the table with its opening towards the audience.

Fill the large cup more than half-way with chocolate milk. Place it on top of the folded bag on the table.

Put a rubber band in your right pocket.

Have the small bowl on the *left* side of the table.

Doing Your Magic:

1. Pick up the large cup in your right hand, and the small cup in the left. Pour milk back and forth into them several times. Then, leave the small cup about half full and put the big cup back on the paper bag.

2. Take the small cup with the first two fingers and the thumb of your right hand. Your thumb should be on the outside. With your left hand, take a big scoop of invisible magic dust from the bowl. Pretend to take a large amount and make a fist over it.

3. Now you have to act. Pretend

DROP
OUTER
SMALL
CUP

SLIDE OUT
BAG WITH
CLOSED FIST

that you need the paper bag, but since your hands are full you don't know how to get it. You can't use your left hand, because it is full of magic dust. You have the small cup by the rim in your right hand. For a second, put the small cup inside the large cup so that you can raise the large cup off the paper bag. This should look like a move to help you get the paper bag. It is really a way to make your secret move.

As you hold the large cup this way, let the outer shell of the small cup drop into the large one. The milk will cushion the sound of the cup dropping. With your left fist still closed, use it to slide the bag out from under the raised cup.

4. Put the large cup down again, on the table. Keep the small cup (now without a bottom and without the chocolate milk) in your fingers.

To free your left hand, sprinkle the invisible magic dust over the bag. Don't tell the audience it's invisible; let them look for it.

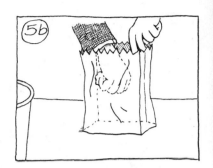

5. Now, with your left hand, shake open the paper bag.

   With your right hand, reach deep into the bag as though you are placing the cup carefully on the bottom. Tell the audience you are trying very hard not to spill any milk. What you are really doing, as soon as your hand is hidden from view, is flattening and folding the cup until it is small enough to sneak out when you remove your hand from the bag.

6. Remove your hand and the hidden cup from the paper bag and reach into your right pocket for a rubber band. Leave the crumpled cup there as you bring out the rubber band.

   Tie the rubber band around the top of the paper bag. Lift it carefully, hold it up, and concentrate. After a moment, open the bag, take out the chocolate bar, crush the bag and toss it to someone in the audience.

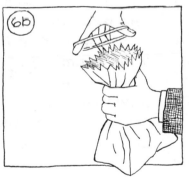

> **Tip:** Treat the paper bag as though the cup of milk were still inside, even after it's gone.

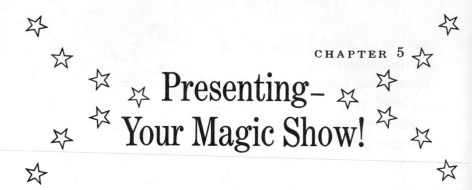

CHAPTER 5

Presenting—Your Magic Show!

Now that you have worked out a fancy name for yourself, and have come up with an image and a costume, and mastered some tricks, you are practically ready to give a show.

A show is more than a display of what you can do. It is time spent with your friends, during which you entertain them. You may be the star, but there is no show—and no star—without an audience. If you are good at what you do, your audience will accept your magic, just as they accept a play or a movie or a TV program—as totally real for the time they are watching it. So give them what they came to see—a good show, and lots of fun.

Work out a program to suit your situation. If are giving your show in the living room, keep your equipment down to a minimum. Don't try to do something with lots of assistants and large props. If you have a whole basement to work in, or a large recreation room, or auditorium, leave out tricks that cannot be seen from far away.

Keep your program short. Your show should be from ten to fifteen minutes long. Ten tricks should be the most to do, and you can do as few as four or five.

Start off with a quick, attention-getting trick which needs no assistants. This lets the audience know what to expect, and shows them how good you are right away.

Your next trick can be a little more involved. Use an assistant if you want to. Tell a story. Let the audience get to know you a little. Have some interesting patter worked out to keep it lively.

Next, you can do a more complicated trick.

THREE THINGS WHICH MAKE
A TRICK EFFECTIVE

timing

naturalness

smoothness of presentation

This one can take longer, because now you have your audience's full attention.

Finish with a quick and colorful trick. Something like THE BROKEN TOOTHPICK is good, especially if you use a bright-colored kerchief. If the last trick in the show is not so colorful, add something of your own. Have your assistant throw a handful of confetti into the air as you take your bow. Substitute bright-colored tissue paper for newspaper on THE AFGHAN BANDS and PAPER RABBITS.

Using just the ten basic tricks and illusions in this book, plus the few warm-ups, you can put together many different programs.

Plan a small show as soon as you have mastered a few tricks. At first, try out your skills on just one or two people. Once you are used to performing in front of others, and can do your magic without mistakes, invite more people to see you. Try not to have the same people twice. The second time around they will be looking for your secrets because they have already seen the magic.

Advertise your Magic Show. This is no time to be shy. Ask an artistic friend to help you make posters, perhaps in return for being one of your assistants.

Make colorful posters with lots of razzmatazz and put them up wherever people pass. If the show is going to be in your living room, put up

HOW TO PREPARE A SHORT PROGRAM

The First Trick

Quick. Dazzling. Surefire. Baffle the audience. Establish your ability as a magician.

Second Trick

Longer. Can involve volunteer or story. Something that will let audience get to know you.

Third Trick

Your feature. Longest or most complicated trick. One that will have astounding effect on audience.

Fourth (Last) Trick

Simple but flashy or colorful. Your grand finale. Short. Fun. Leave audience with good feeling.

posters around the house. If the show is open to the public, put up posters on your tree or fence or in your apartment house lobby, or in shop windows in your neighborhood. If you are giving your show in school, put posters on the bulletin boards. But get permissions first.

The purpose of this advertising is to create ex-

citement about you and interest in your show. The way you advertise yourself will tell people what you think of yourself. Who should know better than you? If you don't think it's sensational, why should they?

John Henry Anderson, a 19th century Scotsman, had two dozen men walk through the streets of London carrying letters three feet high spelling out THE GREAT WIZARD OF THE NORTH, his stage title. This publicity stunt drew quite a crowd to the theater where he was performing. After all, people thought, would he go to all this trouble and expense if he weren't wonderful?

You can make up tickets to be presented at the door. Make your tickets out of colored paper and use different markers to decorate them. Paste gummed stars on them. The time and the place should appear on the tickets, as well as the name of your show. If you are charging admission, print the price on the tickets, too.

Have programs for your audience, listing the tricks you will do and the order in which you will do them. The name of the trick should not give away the surprise. THE MAGICAL MILK-SHAKE, for example, really doesn't give away anything. The surprise will still be there when you do it. Put a program on each seat for the audience.

Keep a copy of the program flat on your performing table, to the side. You can keep track of your place that way.

Arrange the seats ahead of time. Know exactly where you will stand, and where your audience will be. The audience should be directly in front of you, not behind you or to the side.

To open your show, flash or dim the room lights. This brings the audience to attention. An assistant can announce you, and can also walk out with signs introducing each trick as you are about to do it.

If you find that you have stage fright and your mouth goes dry, lick your lips. When your lips are wet, your mouth will get wet and talking will be easier.

When you first get on stage, you may find it

difficult to control all the parts of your body. You will feel awkward. This happens to almost everyone. Press your thumbs into the balls of your middle fingers. You will feel more secure and less fidgety.

Stand in front of a blank wall or curtain so that

you can be seen clearly. Fix the lights so that they are directly on you while the rest of the room and the audience is dim. You can use the light from a slide projector (without slides in it) as a spotlight. Your assistant can play records for background or special effects.

Have something happening all the time. Say things to your audience, between tricks as well as during them. Don't let them fidget while you're setting up your next number. For example, ask the audience a question, like "Do you think I can push this ball through this cup?" or "Are you familiar with the Mystical Eye?"

You should know your moves so well that you never make a mistake. But, if you should, get around it by saying something like "That trick never works well on Monday." Don't give away your error if the audience doesn't catch it. It will spoil the effect of the magic in your whole show.

The curtain call at the end of a show is a "thank you" to your audience. Keep this in mind. Too many performers think it's the other way around and act like show-offs.

The following are some sample routines and programs which you can do with the tricks described in this book. Try to find the best way of presenting the tricks one after another. A few suggestions are given, but work on some of your own.

Make substitutions and changes as you go along, and as you learn new routines. These will give you an idea about how to balance your act, however short or long, and how to fit a program to your time, space, and audience.

From Harry Houdini's
HELPFUL HINTS FOR
YOUNG MAGICIANS UNDER EIGHTY

An old trick well done is far better than a new trick with no effect.

Never tell the audience how good you are; they will soon find that out for themselves.

You may think your trick is old, but it is always new to members of your audience.

Rabbit tricks are positive successes.

When practicing a new trick, try it in front of a looking glass, accompanying your moves with your entire patter.

An old trick in a new dress is always a pleasant change.

Short Program 1

I   THE MAGIC CYLINDER
II   THE GREAT ROPE ESCAPE
III   THE AMAZING CUPS
      AND BALLS
IV   THE PHANTOM
      MONEY BOX

Time: 8-12 minutes
Space: small or average (a room in
   your house, for example)
Audience: small (a few friends and
   family)

For this program, you have to make props ahead of time for numbers I, III, and IV. Notice how the tricks for Program 1 fit the "rules" for making a program, on page 73.

Short Program 2

I   THE BROKEN TOOTHPICK
II   THE MYSTICAL EYE
III THE MAGICAL MILKSHAKE
IV MAGIC SPELLING

Time: 8-12 minutes
Space: small or average
Audience: large (more than 10
    people)

With a lot of people and a small amount of room, you have people crowded around you, watching every move. The best thing is to use them in your act. Call on them as volunteers and to take part in some of the routines. At the same time, keep them in their seats. In tricks I and II, you can go *to* the audience for help. In III, someone has to come up for a moment only. In IV, the audience can spell along with you, from their seats.

Short Program 3

I   THE MAGIC CYLINDER
II THE PHANTOM
    MONEY BOX
III MAGIC SPELLING
IV THE AMAZING CUPS
    AND BALLS
V   THE BROKEN TOOTHPICK

Time: 8-10 minutes
Space: small
Audience: any size

This program works well in a small space, for any number of people, as long as they can see what you are doing with your hands from where they sit.

Average Program 4

I THE MAGIC CYLINDER
II THE MYSTICAL EYE
III THE RUBBER PENCIL
IV MAGIC SPELLING
V THE AMAZING CUPS
AND BALLS
VI THE BROKEN TOOTHPICK

Time: 8-10 minutes
Space: small
Audience: small

Program 4 concentrates on close-up magic. Your magic must be seen close-up or some of the details will not be seen at all.

Seat your audience a little closer to you than usual for this one.

There is a little more room for talking with your audience in this program. See if you can come up with a theme or main story to link all the tricks together.

Average Program 5

    I   THE   MAGIC   CYLINDER
    II   THE   BROKEN   TOOTHPICK
    III   THE   AMAZING   CUPS
          AND BALLS
    IV   THE   AFGHAN   BANDS
    V   THE   PHANTOM
          MONEY BOX
    VI   MAGIC   SPELLING

Time: 8-12 minutes
Space: Average
Audience: Average

You may want to try THE AFGHAN
BANDS with bright-colored tissue paper
instead of newspaper. It's more colorful
and the twists in the bands are not that
easy to see.

As a matter of fact, this is a good
program for testing how well you can
design. Your Magic Cylinder and Phantom Money Box can be designed alike,
maybe in silver, or gold, with black symbols, or painted bright red and shel-
lacked, to give them a super-special
appearance.

Average Program 6

I   THE PHANTOM
       MONEY BOX
II   THE PAPER RACE
III   CUTTING SOMEONE
       IN HALF
IV   THE MAGICAL MILKSHAKE
V   THE MYSTICAL EYE
VI   THE BROKEN TOOTHPICK

Time: 10-15 minutes
Space: large
Audience: any size

With more space to move around in, you can do II and III with more ease. When you call up your volunteers for II, III, and IV, there will be room for them to walk up and join you.

Long Program 7

I THE BROKEN TOOTHPICK
II THE MAGIC CYLINDER
III THE PHANTOM
MONEY BOX
IV EGG SPINNERS
V THE AMAZING CUPS
AND BALLS
VI THE MYSTICAL EYE
VII CUTTING SOMEONE
IN HALF
VIII THE AFGHAN BANDS

Time: 10-15 minutes
Space: large
Audience: any size

In a longer program, it is important to put a couple of things in that are pure entertainment and relief. That goes for you as well as for your audience. Numbers I, II, and III are fun to do, but take a lot of work and concentration. Therefore, number IV is a relaxer, a bit of fun for you, before you resume your magic tricks.

The AFGHAN BANDS, although not a real part of your magic act, is right for the end of this show because it lets the audience down slowly after a sensational and long act.

Long Program 8

Time: 15 minutes
Space: large
Audience: any size

In this program, you will notice that a couple of warm-ups have been planted in between the tricks for relief. Although there is really no "magic" involved in these, they seem to fit the situation. It would be even better if you could tie them to your routine through your patter.

For example, as you make the paper tree, you might start a story about looking for a wise man who would teach you some ancient magic. After searching far and wide for many years, you found the wise man, who told you that you would find your ancient magic under a repapswen tree.

Again, you searched around the world and couldn't find such a tree. You found yew and mulberry, bamboo and ginkgo and mesquite, spruce and juniper—but never the repapswen.

Then, one day, as you were reading your book of magic spells backwards (all magic is printed backwards) you discovered the repapswen tree, on page 2,348! Spelled frontwards, it was NEWSPAPER TREE. (By the time you get to this point in your story, you should have the tree about four or five feet tall.)

And right underneath the instructions for the repapswen, or newspaper, tree, were the instructions for an ancient magic trick: THE AMAZING CUPS AND BALLS.

The wise man was right! You found your ancient magic under a repapswen tree!

So, you see, the paper tree leads naturally into the AMAZING CUPS AND BALLS. You can carry the same routine a little farther, or you can start with new patter now.

Long Program 9

Part I

I THE PAPER RACE
II THE SAUSAGE ON THE
END OF YOUR NOSE
III THE AMAZING CUPS
AND BALLS
IV CUTTING SOMEONE
IN HALF

Intermission

Part II

V THE PHANTOM MONEY
BOX
VI MAGIC SPELLING
VII THE FLOATING BODY
VIII THE MAGICAL MILKSHAKE

Time: 20 minutes (including 5-minute
intermission)
Space: large
Audience: large

Program 9 requires quite a bit of mastery before you can attempt it. You can begin your show with an example of a trick and an illusion. Number I is an example of a trick—it works because it is set up in advance to *look* magical. Number II is an illusion because your eyes play the trick here.

The audience will be involved right away with this warm-up. Numbers III and IV are larger versions of tricks and illusions.

If you are giving your show in a place where you can leave the room or stage for a few minutes without having your props handled closely by the audience, you can have an intermission. In this case, treat the first half of the show as a show in itself, but the second half as an even more spectacular one.

When trying to balance a program, break it up into sections this way, even without an intermission. The first four or five tricks make up one small show, the next few tricks another small show. Have your biggest feature toward the end of the second half.

MAGIC DEALERS

Consult your local *Yellow Pages* for magic dealers in your area. Look under "Magicians' Supplies." If you must shop by mail, many dealers have catalogs listing a great variety of tricks and illusions that are packaged with instructions and suggestions. These make interesting reference material and are fun to have in your magic collection. But they usually cost money. Inquire before you order a catalog. Some prices are indicated below, but they may change at any time. For orders outside the United States, prices are usually higher.

Abbotts Magic Co.
124 St. Joseph
Colon, Michigan 49040
Catalog—$7.50

Abracadabra Magic Shop
Dept. C-457
P.O. Box 463
Scotch Plains, New Jersey 07076
Catalog—$1.00 postpaid

Balloon and Magic Store
2050 Boston Avenue
Bridgeport, Connecticut 06610
Write for Catalog

Eagle Magic Store
708 Portland Avenue
Minneapolis, Minnesota 55415
Catalog—$2.00

Hank Lee's Magic Factory
P.O. Box 1359
Boston, Massachusetts 02111
Catalog—$5.00

Hornmann Magic Co.
45 West 34th St.
Suite 607
New York, New York 10001
Catalog—$2.00

Louis Tannen, Inc.
6 West 32nd
New York, New York 10001
Catalog—$8.00

Magic Inc.
5082 North Lincoln Avenue
Chicago, Illinois 60625
General Catalog—$5.00
Book Catalog—$2.00

Magicland
3767 Forest Lane
Suite 100
Dallas, Texas 75244
Free Catalogs
Magic tricks or disguises

Martinka Co.
45 West 34th Street
Suite 607
New York, New York 10001
Collector's catalog

Mecca Magic
49 Dodd
Bloomfield, New Jersey 07003
3 Catalog packages available:
$2.00, $5.00, and $10.00

Stevens Magic Emporium
3238 East Douglas
Wichita, Kansas 67208
Catalog — $2.50

MAGIC MAGAZINES

GENII, The International Conjurors' Magazine, published by William Larser, Jr., one of the creators of the famous Magic Castle in Hollywood, a meeting place for international magicians. $25.00 per year. Genii Publications. 7001 Franklin Avenue, Los Angeles, California 90028.

TOPS, published by Abbott's Magic Co., 124 St. Joseph, Colon, Michigan 49040. $1.50 per issue; $3.00 for September's All-Trick Issue; $15.00 yearly.

BOOKS ABOUT STAGE MAGIC

The First Book of Magic, by Edward Stoddard. Published by Franklin Watts, Inc., 1953.

Fun with Magic, by Joseph Leeming. Published by J. Lippincott Company, 1943.

Magic in Your Pockets, by Bill Severn. Published by David McKay Co., Inc., 1964.

Magic Shows You Can Give, by Bill Severn. Published by David McKay Co., Inc., 1965.

Magic Tricks, by Guy Fredericks. Published by Young Readers Press.

Magic with Paper, by Bill Severn. Published by David McKay Co., Inc.

Mixed Bag of Magic Tricks, by Roz Abisch and Boche Kaplan. Published by Walker and Company, 1973.

Secrets of Magic, by Walter Gibson. Published by Grosset & Dunlap, 1967.

Index